Let's Play!

Judi Laman

Literacy Consultants
David Booth • Kathleen Corrigan

Sports can be played
in all different seasons.

It can be hard to choose
what to play.
The time of year can help.

You can ski or snowboard
if you live in a place
where there is snow.

You can surf if you live
in a place with big waves.

Baseball is a sport
to play in summer.
It is played in spring
and fall too.
Baseball is played outside.

Two teams play.
Players try to hit
and catch a ball.
They run around bases
to score points.

Basketball can be played
all year round.
It can be played outside
when the weather is warm.
It can be played inside
if the weather is cold.

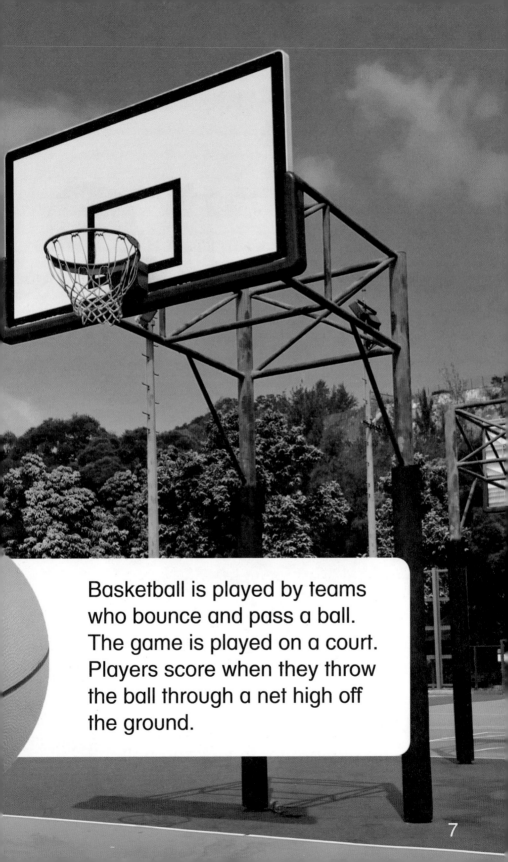

Basketball is played by teams who bounce and pass a ball. The game is played on a court. Players score when they throw the ball through a net high off the ground.

Soccer is a sport
that is played on a grass field.
The players try to kick the ball
into a net.

Soccer is played when
there is no snow on the ground.
Some people play soccer inside too.
They can play soccer in winter.

Track and field has
many different events.
It has short races.
It has long races.
It has jumping and
throwing too.

Most track and field events
take place outside.
It is good to have weather
that is not too hot or too cold.
Track and field events
can take place indoors too.

Swimming can be done
outside in warm weather.
It can be done indoors
all year long.

Some people swim in races.
Some people swim
to have fun in the water.
Some people do dances
in the water with a team.

Skiing is a sport that people can do in winter.
People wear warm clothes and boots with skis to zoom down snowy hills.

People can also ice skate
when it is cold outside.
They can skate on a frozen pond.
They can make a rink to skate on
when the air is very cold.
Some ice rinks are inside.

There are many sports
that you can play
in spring, summer,
fall, and winter.

What sports do you like to play
in each of the seasons?

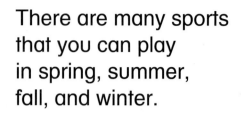